The Awful Rowing
Toward God

Also by Anne Sexton

To Bedlam and Part Way Back
All My Pretty Ones
Live or Die
Love Poems
Transformations
The Book of Folly
The Death Notebooks

The
Awful Rowing
Toward God

Anne Sexton

Houghton Mifflin Company Boston

Some of the poems in this book have appeared in *American Poetry Review, Boston University Journal, Contrasts* (Britain), *Georgia Review, Ms. Magazine, Mundus Artium, The New Republic* and *Paris Review*.

"Riding the Elevator Into the Sky" originally appeared in *The New Yorker* in June 1974.

w 10 9 8 7 6 5 4 3

Library of Congress Cataloging in Publication Data

Sexton, Anne.
    The awful rowing toward God.

    Poems.
    I. Title.
PS3537.E915A95   811'.5'4   74-23618
ISBN 0-395-20365-1   ISBN 0-395-20366-X pbk.

Printed in the United States of America

For Brother Dennis, wherever he is,
and for James Wright, who would know.

"When the heavens are obscured to us, and nothing noble or heroic appears, but we are oppressed by imperfection and shortcoming on all hands, we are apt to suck our thumbs and decry our fates. As if nothing were to be done in cloudy weather, or, if heaven were not accessible by the upper road, men would not find out a lower . . . There are two ways to victory, — to strive bravely, or to yield. How much pain the last will save we have not yet learned."

HENRY DAVID THOREAU

Sören Kierkegaard says, "But above all do not make yourself important by doubting."

The days, like great black oxen tread the world;
God the herdsman goads them from behind,
And I am broken by their passing feet.

—A poet quoting a poet to a poet

CONTENTS

1   Rowing

3   The Civil War

5   The Children

7   Two Hands

9   The Room of My Life

11   The Witch's Life

13   The Earth Falls Down

15   Courage

17   Riding the Elevator Into the Sky

19   When Man Enters Woman

20   The Fish That Walked

22   The Fallen Angels

24   The Earth

26   After Auschwitz

28   The Poet of Ignorance

30   The Sermon of the Twelve Acknowledgments

34   The Evil Eye

36   The Dead Heart

38   The Play

40   The Sickness Unto Death

42   Locked Doors

44   The Evil Seekers

46   The Wall

48   Is It True?

58 Welcome Morning

60 Jesus, the Actor, Plays the Holy Ghost

62 The God-Monger

64 What the Bird with the Human Head Knew

66 The Fire Thief

69 The Big Heart

71 Words

72 Mothers

74 Doctors

76 Frenzy

77 Snow

78 Small Wire

79 The Saints Come Marching In

83 Not So. Not So.

85 The Rowing Endeth

The Awful Rowing Toward God

ROWING

A story, a story!
(Let it go. Let it come.)
I was stamped out like a Plymouth fender
into this world.
First came the crib
with its glacial bars.
Then dolls
and the devotion to their plastic mouths.
Then there was school,
the little straight rows of chairs,
blotting my name over and over,
but undersea all the time,
a stranger whose elbows wouldn't work.
Then there was life
with its cruel houses
and people who seldom touched —
though touch is all —
but I grew,
like a pig in a trenchcoat I grew,
and then there were many strange apparitions,
the nagging rain, the sun turning into poison
and all of that, saws working through my heart,
but I grew, I grew,
and God was there like an island I had not rowed to,
still ignorant of Him, my arms and my legs worked,
and I grew, I grew,

I wore rubies and bought tomatoes
and now, in my middle age,
about nineteen in the head I'd say,
I am rowing, I am rowing
though the oarlocks stick and are rusty
and the sea blinks and rolls
like a worried eyeball,
but I am rowing, I am rowing,
though the wind pushes me back
and I know that that island will not be perfect,
it will have the flaws of life,
the absurdities of the dinner table,
but there will be a door
and I will open it
and I will get rid of the rat inside of me,
the gnawing pestilential rat.
God will take it with his two hands
and embrace it.

As the African says:
This is my tale which I have told,
if it be sweet, if it be not sweet,
take somewhere else and let some return to me.
This story ends with me still rowing.

THE CIVIL WAR

I am torn in two
but I will conquer myself.
I will dig up the pride.
I will take scissors
and cut out the beggar.
I will take a crowbar
and pry out the broken
pieces of God in me.
Just like a jigsaw puzzle,
I will put Him together again
with the patience of a chess player.

How many pieces?

It feels like thousands,
God dressed up like a whore
in a slime of green algae.
God dressed up like an old man
staggering out of His shoes.
God dressed up like a child,
all naked,
even without skin,
soft as an avocado when you peel it.
And others, others, others.

But I will conquer them all
and build a whole nation of God

in me — but united,
build a new soul,
dress it with skin
and then put on my shirt
and sing an anthem,
a song of myself.

THE CHILDREN

The children are all crying in their pens
and the surf carries their cries away.
They are old men who have seen too much,
their mouths are full of dirty clothes,
the tongues poverty, tears like pus.
The surf pushes their cries back.
Listen.
They are bewitched.
They are writing down their life
on the wings of an elf
who then dissolves.
They are writing down their life
on a century fallen to ruin.
They are writing down their life
on the bomb of an alien God.
I am too.

We must get help.
The children are dying in their pens.
Their bodies are crumbling.
Their tongues are twisting backwards.
There is a certain ritual to it.
There is a dance they do in their pens.
Their mouths are immense.
They are swallowing monster hearts.
So is my mouth.

Listen.
We must all stop dying in the little ways,
in the craters of hate,
in the potholes of indifference —
a murder in the temple.
The place I live in
is a kind of maze
and I keep seeking
the exit or the home.
Yet if I could listen
to the bulldog courage of those children
and turn inward into the plague of my soul
with more eyes than the stars
I could melt the darkness —
as suddenly as that time
when an awful headache goes away
or someone puts out the fire —
and stop the darkness and its amputations
and find the real McCoy
in the private holiness
of my hands.

TWO HANDS

From the sea came a hand,
ignorant as a penny,
troubled with the salt of its mother,
mute with the silence of the fishes,
quick with the altars of the tides,
and God reached out of His mouth
and called it man.
Up came the other hand
and God called it woman.
The hands applauded.
And this was no sin.
It was as it was meant to be.

I see them roaming the streets:
Levi complaining about his mattress,
Sarah studying a beetle,
Mandrake holding his coffee mug,
Sally playing the drum at a football game,
John closing the eyes of the dying woman,
and some who are in prison,
even the prison of their bodies,
as Christ was prisoned in His body
until the triumph came.

Unwind, hands,
you angel webs,

unwind like the coil of a jumping jack,
cup together and let yourselves fill up with sun
and applaud, world,
applaud.

THE ROOM OF MY LIFE

Here,
in the room of my life
the objects keep changing.
Ashtrays to cry into,
the suffering brother of the wood walls,
the forty-eight keys of the typewriter
each an eyeball that is never shut,
the books, each a contestant in a beauty contest,
the black chair, a dog coffin made of Naugahyde,
the sockets on the wall
waiting like a cave of bees,
the gold rug
a conversation of heels and toes,
the fireplace
a knife waiting for someone to pick it up,
the sofa, exhausted with the exertion of a whore,
the phone
two flowers taking root in its crotch,
the doors
opening and closing like sea clams,
the lights
poking at me,
lighting up both the soil and the laugh.
The windows,
the starving windows
that drive the trees like nails into my heart.

Each day I feed the world out there
although birds explode
right and left.
I feed the world in here too,
offering the desk puppy biscuits.
However, nothing is just what it seems to be.
My objects dream and wear new costumes,
compelled to, it seems, by all the words in my hands
and the sea that bangs in my throat.

THE WITCH'S LIFE

When I was a child
there was an old woman in our neighborhood
whom we called The Witch.
All day she peered from her second story window
from behind the wrinkled curtains
and sometimes she would open the window
and yell: Get out of my life!
She had hair like kelp
and a voice like a boulder.

I think of her sometimes now
and wonder if I am becoming her.
My shoes turn up like a jester's.
Clumps of my hair, as I write this,
curl up individually like toes.
I am shoveling the children out,
scoop after scoop.
Only my books anoint me,
and a few friends,
those who reach into my veins.
Maybe I am becoming a hermit,
opening the door for only
a few special animals?
Maybe my skull is too crowded
and it has no opening through which
to feed it soup?

11

Maybe I have plugged up my sockets
to keep the gods in?
Maybe, although my heart
is a kitten of butter,
I am blowing it up like a zeppelin.
Yes. It is the witch's life,
climbing the primordial climb,
a dream within a dream,
then sitting here
holding a basket of fire.

THE EARTH FALLS DOWN

If I could blame it all on the weather,
the snow like the cadaver's table,
the trees turned into knitting needles,
the ground as hard as a frozen haddock,
the pond wearing its mustache of frost.
If I could blame conditions on *that*,
if I could blame the hearts of strangers
striding muffled down the street,
or blame the dogs, every color,
sniffing each other
and pissing on the doorstep . . .
If I could blame the war on the war
where its fire Brillos my hair . . .
If I could blame the bosses
and the presidents for
their unpardonable songs . . .
If I could blame it on all
the mothers and fathers of the world,
they of the lessons, the pellets of power,
they of the love surrounding you like batter . . .
Blame it on God perhaps?
He of the first opening
that pushed us all into our first mistakes?
No, I'll blame it on Man
For Man is God
and man is eating the earth up

like a candy bar
and not one of them can be left alone with the ocean
for it is known he will gulp it all down.
The stars (possibly) are safe.
At least for the moment.
The stars are pears
that no one can reach,
even for a wedding.

Perhaps for a death.

COURAGE

It is in the small things we see it.
The child's first step,
as awesome as an earthquake.
The first time you rode a bike,
wallowing up the sidewalk.
The first spanking when your heart
went on a journey all alone.
When they called you crybaby
or poor or fatty or crazy
and made you into an alien,
you drank their acid
and concealed it.

Later,
if you faced the death of bombs and bullets
you did not do it with a banner,
you did it with only a hat to
cover your heart.
You did not fondle the weakness inside you
though it was there.
Your courage was a small coal
that you kept swallowing.
If your buddy saved you
and died himself in so doing,
then his courage was not courage,
it was love; love as simple as shaving soap.

Later,
if you have endured a great despair,
then you did it alone,
getting a transfusion from the fire,
picking the scabs off your heart,
then wringing it out like a sock.
Next, my kinsman, you powdered your sorrow,
you gave it a back rub
and then you covered it with a blanket
and after it had slept a while
it woke to the wings of the roses
and was transformed.

Later,
when you face old age and its natural conclusion
your courage will still be shown in the little ways,
each spring will be a sword you'll sharpen,
those you love will live in a fever of love,
and you'll bargain with the calendar
and at the last moment
when death opens the back door
you'll put on your carpet slippers
and stride out.

RIDING THE ELEVATOR INTO
THE SKY

As the fireman said:
Don't book a room over the fifth floor
in any hotel in New York.
They have ladders that will reach further
but no one will climb them.
As the New York *Times* said:
The elevator always seeks out
the floor of the fire
and automatically opens
and won't shut.
These are the warnings
that you must forget
if you're climbing out of yourself.
If you're going to smash into the sky.

Many times I've gone past
the fifth floor,
cranking upward,
but only once
have I gone all the way up.
Sixtieth floor:
small plants and swans bending
into their grave.
Floor two hundred:
mountains with the patience of a cat,
silence wearing its sneakers.

Floor five hundred:
messages and letters centuries old,
birds to drink,
a kitchen of clouds.
Floor six thousand:
the stars,
skeletons on fire,
their arms singing.
And a key,
a very large key,
that opens something —
some useful door —
somewhere —
up there.

WHEN MAN ENTERS WOMAN

When man
enters woman,
like the surf biting the shore,
again and again,
and the woman opens her mouth in pleasure
and her teeth gleam
like the alphabet,
Logos appears milking a star,
and the man
inside of woman
ties a knot
so that they will
never again be separate
and the woman
climbs into a flower
and swallows its stem
and Logos appears
and unleashes their rivers.

This man,
this woman
with their double hunger,
have tried to reach through
the curtain of God
and briefly they have,
though God
in His perversity
unties the knot.

THE FISH THAT WALKED

Up from oysters
and the confused weeds,
out from the tears of God,
the wounding tides,
he came.
He became a hunter of roots
and breathed like a man.
He ruffled through the grasses
and became known to the sky.
I stood close and watched it all.
Beg pardon, he said
but you have skin divers,
you have hooks and nets,
so why shouldn't I
enter your element for a moment?
Though it is curious here,
unusually awkward to walk.
It is without grace.
There is no rhythm
in this country of dirt.

And I said to him:
From some country
that I have misplaced
I can recall a few things . . .
but the light of the kitchen

gets in the way.
Yet there was a dance
when I kneaded the bread
there was a song my mother
used to sing . . .
And the salt of God's belly
where I floated in a cup of darkness.
I long for your country, fish.

The fish replied:
You must be a poet,
a lady of evil luck
desiring to be what you are not,
longing to be
what you can only visit.

THE FALLEN ANGELS

"Who are they"
"Fallen angels who were not good enough to be saved,
nor bad enough to be lost" say the peasantry.

They come on to my clean
sheet of paper and leave a Rorschach blot.
They do not do this to be mean,
they do it to give me a sign
they want me, as Aubrey Beardsley once said,
to shove it around till something comes.
Clumsy as I am,
I do it.
For I am like them —
both saved and lost,
tumbling downward like Humpty Dumpty
off the alphabet.

Each morning I push them off my bed
and when they get in the salad
rolling in it like a dog,
I pick each one out
just the way my daughter
picks out the anchovies.
In May they dance on the jonquils,
wearing out their toes,
laughing like fish.
In November,
the dread month,

they suck the childhood out of the berries
and turn them sour and inedible.

Yet they keep me company.
They wiggle up life.
They pass out their magic
like Assorted Lifesavers.
They go with me to the dentist
and protect me from the drill.
At the same time,
they go to class with me
and lie to my students.

O fallen angel,
the companion within me,
whisper something holy
before you pinch me
into the grave.

THE EARTH

God loafs around heaven,
without a shape
but He would like to smoke His cigar
or bite His fingernails
and so forth.

God owns heaven
but He craves the earth,
the earth with its little sleepy caves,
its bird resting at the kitchen window,
even its murders lined up like broken chairs,
even its writers digging into their souls
with jackhammers,
even its hucksters selling their animals
for gold,
even its babies sniffing for their music,
the farm house, white as a bone,
sitting in the lap of its corn,
even the statue holding up its widowed life,
even the ocean with its cupful of students,
but most of all He envies the bodies,
He who has no body.

The eyes, opening and shutting like keyholes
and never forgetting, recording by thousands,
the skull with its brains like eels —

the tablet of the world —
the bones and their joints
that build and break for any trick,
the genitals,
the ballast of the eternal,
and the heart, of course,
that swallows the tides
and spits them out cleansed.

He does not envy the soul so much.
He is all soul
but He would like to house it in a body
and come down
and give it a bath
now and then.

AFTER AUSCHWITZ

Anger,
as black as a hook,
overtakes me.
Each day,
each Nazi
took, at 8:00 A.M., a baby
and sautéed him for breakfast
in his frying pan.

And death looks on with a casual eye
and picks at the dirt under his fingernail.

Man is evil,
I say aloud.
Man is a flower
that should be burnt,
I say aloud.
Man
is a bird full of mud,
I say aloud.

And death looks on with a casual eye
and scratches his anus.

Man with his small pink toes,
with his miraculous fingers

is not a temple
but an outhouse,
I say aloud.
Let man never again raise his teacup.
Let man never again write a book.
Let man never again put on his shoe.
Let man never again raise his eyes,
on a soft July night.
Never. Never. Never. Never. Never.
I say these things aloud.

I beg the Lord not to hear.

THE POET OF IGNORANCE

Perhaps the earth is floating,
I do not know.
Perhaps the stars are little paper cutups
made by some giant scissors,
I do not know.
Perhaps the moon is a frozen tear,
I do not know.
Perhaps God is only a deep voice
heard by the deaf,
I do not know.

Perhaps I am no one.
True, I have a body
and I cannot escape from it.
I would like to fly out of my head,
but that is out of the question.
It is written on the tablet of destiny
that I am stuck here in this human form.
That being the case
I would like to call attention to my problem.

There is an animal inside me,
clutching fast to my heart,
a huge crab.
The doctors of Boston
have thrown up their hands.

They have tried scalpels,
needles, poison gasses and the like.
The crab remains.
It is a great weight.
I try to forget it, go about my business,
cook the broccoli, open and shut books,
brush my teeth and tie my shoes.
I have tried prayer
but as I pray the crab grips harder
and the pain enlarges.

I had a dream once,
perhaps it was a dream,
that the crab was my ignorance of God.
But who am I to believe in dreams?

THE SERMON OF THE TWELVE ACKNOWLEDGMENTS

January?
The month is dumb.
It is fraudulent.
It does not cleanse itself.
The hens lay blood-stained eggs.
Do not lend your bread to anyone
lest it nevermore rise.
Do not eat lentils or your hair will fall out.

Do not rely on February
except when your cat has kittens,
throbbing into the snow.
Do not use knives and forks
unless there is a thaw,
like the yawn of a baby.
The sun in this month
begets a headache
like an angel slapping you in the face.

Earthquakes mean March.
The dragon will move,
and the earth will open like a wound.
There will be great rain or snow
so save some coal for your uncle.
The sun of this month cures all.
Therefore, old women say:

Let the sun of March shine on my daughter,
but let the sun of February shine on my daughter-in-law.
However, if you go to a party
dressed as the anti-Christ
you will be frozen to death by morning.

During the rainstorms of April
the oyster rises from the sea
and opens its shell —
rain enters it —
when it sinks the raindrops
become the pearl.
So take a picnic,
open your body,
and give birth to pearls.

June and July?
These are the months
we call Boiling Water.
There is sweat on the cat but the grape
marries herself to the sun.

Hesitate in August.
Be shy.
Let your toes tremble in their sandals.
However, pick the grape
and eat with confidence.
The grape is the blood of God.
Watch out when holding a knife
or you will behead St. John the Baptist.

Touch the Cross in September,
knock on it three times

and say aloud the name of the Lord.
Put seven bowls of salt on the roof overnight
and the next morning the damp one
will foretell the month of rain.
Do not faint in September
or you will wake up in a dead city.

If someone dies in October
do not sweep the house for three days
or the rest of you will go.
Also do not step on a boy's head
for the devil will enter your ears
like music.

November?
Shave,
whether you have hair or not.
Hair is not good,
nothing is allowed to grow,
all is allowed to die.
Because nothing grows
you may be tempted to count the stars
but beware,
in November counting the stars
gives you boils.
Beware of tall people,
they will go mad.
Don't harm the turtle dove
because he is a great shoe
that has swallowed Christ's blood.

December?
On December fourth

water spurts out of the mouse.
Put herbs in its eyes and boil corn
and put the corn away for the night
so that the Lord may trample on it
and bring you luck.
For many days the Lord has been
shut up in the oven.
After that He is boiled,
but He never dies, never dies.

THE EVIL EYE

It comes oozing
out of flowers at night,
it comes out of the rain
if a snake looks skyward,
it comes out of chairs and tables
if you don't point at them and say their names.
It comes into your mouth while you sleep,
pressing in like a washcloth.
Beware. Beware.

If you meet a cross-eyed person
you must plunge into the grass,
alongside the chilly ants,
fish through the green fingernails
and come up with the four-leaf clover
or your blood will congeal
like cold gravy.

If you run across a horseshoe,
passerby,
stop, take your hands out of your pockets
and count the nails
as you count your children
or your money.
Otherwise a sand flea will crawl in your ear
and fly into your brain

and the only way you'll keep from going mad
is to be hit with a hammer every hour.

If a hunchback is in the elevator with you
don't turn away,
immediately touch his hump
for his child will be born from his back tomorrow
and if he promptly bites the baby's nails off
(so it won't become a thief)
that child will be holy
and you, simple bird that you are,
may go on flying.

When you knock on wood,
and you do,
you knock on the Cross
and Jesus gives you a fragment of His body
and breaks an egg in your toilet,
giving up one life
for one life.

THE DEAD HEART

After I wrote this, a friend scrawled on this page, "Yes."

And I said, merely to myself, "I wish it could be for a different seizure — as with Molly Bloom with her 'and yes I said yes I will Yes.' "

It is not a turtle
hiding in its little green shell.
It is not a stone
to pick up and put under your black wing.
It is not a subway car that is obsolete.
It is not a lump of coal that you could light.
It is a dead heart.
It is inside of me.
It is a stranger
yet once it was agreeable,
opening and closing like a clam.

What it has cost me you can't imagine,
shrinks, priests, lovers, children, husbands,
friends and all the lot.
An expensive thing it was to keep going.
It gave back too.
Don't deny it!
I half wonder if April would bring it back to life?
A tulip? The first bud?
But those are just musings on my part,
the pity one has when one looks at a cadaver.

How did it die?
I called it EVIL.

I said to it, your poems stink like vomit.
I didn't stay to hear the last sentence.
It died on the word EVIL.
I did it with my tongue.
The tongue, the Chinese say,
is like a sharp knife:
it kills
without drawing blood.

THE PLAY

I am the only actor.
It is difficult for one woman
to act out a whole play.
The play is my life,
my solo act.
My running after the hands
and never catching up.
(The hands are out of sight —
that is, offstage.)
All I am doing onstage is running,
running to keep up,
but never making it.

Suddenly I stop running.
(This moves the plot along a bit.)
I give speeches, hundreds,
all prayers, all soliloquies.
I say absurd things like:
eggs must not quarrel with stones
or, keep your broken arm inside your sleeve
or, I am standing upright
but my shadow is crooked.
And such and such.
Many boos. Many boos.

Despite that I go on to the last lines:
To be without God is to be a snake

who wants to swallow an elephant.
The curtain falls.
The audience rushes out.
It was a bad performance.
That's because I'm the only actor
and there are few humans whose lives
will make an interesting play.
Don't you agree?

THE SICKNESS UNTO DEATH

God went out of me
as if the sea dried up like sandpaper,
as if the sun became a latrine.
God went out of my fingers.
They became stone.
My body became a side of mutton
and despair roamed the slaughterhouse.

Someone brought me oranges in my despair
but I could not eat a one
for God was in that orange.
I could not touch what did not belong to me.
The priest came,
he said God was even in Hitler.
I did not believe him
for if God were in Hitler
then God would be in me.
I did not hear the bird sounds.
They had left.
I did not see the speechless clouds,
I saw only the little white dish of my faith
breaking in the crater.
I kept saying:
I've got to have something to hold on to.
People gave me Bibles, crucifixes,
a yellow daisy,

but I could not touch them,
I who was a house full of bowel movement,
I who was a defaced altar,
I who wanted to crawl toward God
could not move nor eat bread.

So I ate myself,
bite by bite,
and the tears washed me,
wave after cowardly wave,
swallowing canker after canker
and Jesus stood over me looking down
and He laughed to find me gone,
and put His mouth to mine
and gave me His air.

My kindred, my brother, I said
and gave the yellow daisy
to the crazy woman in the next bed.

LOCKED DOORS

For the angels who inhabit this town,
although their shape constantly changes,
each night we leave some cold potatoes
and a bowl of milk on the windowsill.
Usually they inhabit heaven where,
by the way, no tears are allowed.
They push the moon around like
a boiled yam.
The Milky Way is their hen
with her many children.
When it is night the cows lie down
but the moon, that big bull,
stands up.

However, there is a locked room up there
with an iron door that can't be opened.
It has all your bad dreams in it.
It is hell.
Some say the devil locks the door
from the inside.
Some say the angels lock it from
the outside.
The people inside have no water
and are never allowed to touch.
They crack like macadam.
They are mute.

They do not cry help
except inside
where their hearts are covered with grubs.

I would like to unlock that door,
turn the rusty key
and hold each fallen one in my arms
but I cannot, I cannot.
I can only sit here on earth
at my place at the table.

THE EVIL SEEKERS

We are born with luck
which is to say with gold in our mouth.
As new and smooth as a grape,
as pure as a pond in Alaska,
as good as the stem of a green bean —
we are born and that ought to be enough,
we ought to be able to carry on from that
but one must learn about evil,
learn what is subhuman,
learn how the blood pops out like a scream,
one must see the night
before one can realize the day,
one must listen hard to the animal within,
one must walk like a sleepwalker
on the edge of the roof,
one must throw some part of her body
into the devil's mouth.
Odd stuff, you'd say.
But I'd say
you must die a little,
have a book of matches go off in your hand,
see your best friend copying your exam,
visit an Indian reservation and see
their plastic feathers,
the dead dream.
One must be a prisoner just once to hear

the lock twist into his gut.
After all that
one is free to grasp at the trees, the stones,
the sky, the birds that make sense out of air.
But even in a telephone booth
evil can seep out of the receiver
and we must cover it with a mattress,
and then tear it from its roots
and bury it,
bury it.

THE WALL

Nature is full of teeth
that come in one by one, then
decay,
fall out.
In nature nothing is stable,
all is change, bears, dogs, peas, the willow,
all disappear. Only to be reborn.
Rocks crumble, make new forms,
oceans move the continents,
mountains rise up and down like ghosts
yet all is natural, all is change.

As I write this sentence
about one hundred and four generations
since Christ, nothing has changed
except knowledge, the test tube.
Man still falls into the dirt
and is covered.
As I write this sentence one thousand are going
and one thousand are coming.
It is like the well that never dries up.
It is like the sea which is the kitchen of God.

We are all earthworms,
digging into our wrinkles.
We live beneath the ground

and if Christ should come in the form of a plow
and dig a furrow and push us up into the day
we earthworms would be blinded by the sudden light
and writhe in our distress.
As I write this sentence I too writhe.

For all you who are going,
and there are many who are climbing their pain,
many who will be painted out with a black ink
suddenly and before it is time,
for those many I say,
awkwardly, clumsily,
take off your life like trousers,
your shoes, your underwear,
then take off your flesh,
unpick the lock of your bones.
In other words
take off the wall
that separates you from God.

IS IT TRUE?

Once more
the sun roaming on the carpenter's back
as he puts joist to sill
and then occasionally he looks to the sky
as even the hen when it drinks
looks toward heaven.
Once in Rome I knelt in front of the Pope
as he waved from his high window.
It was because of a pain in my bowels.
Occasionally the devil has crawled
in and out of me,
through my cigarettes I suppose,
my passionate habit.

Now even the promised land of
Israel has a Hilton
and many tall buildings.
Perhaps it is true,
just as the sun passes over filth
and is not defiled.
For this reason I can book a room in a Hilton
or its terrible playfellow The Holiday Inn
though I never know what city I'm in when I wake up.
I have lost my map
and Jesus has squeezed out of the Gideon,
down to the bar for pretzels and a beer.

Today the Supreme Court made abortion legal.
Bless them.
Bless all women
who want to remake their own likeness
but not every day.
Bless the woman who took the cop's gun.
Bless also the woman who gave it back.
Bless woman for the apple she married.
Bless woman for her brain cells, little cell-computers.
Is it true?
Is it true?

Hare krishna, hare krishna,
krishna, krishna, hare hare
hare rama hare rama
rama rama hare,
they sing on the streets of Harvard Square,
tinkling their little thumb cymbals
and reed pipes, dancing with their joy.
They know what they know.

When I tell the priest I am evil
he asks for a definition of the word.
Do you mean sin? he asks.
Sin, hell! I reply.
I've committed every one.
What I mean is evil,
(not meaning to be, you understand,
just something I ate).
Evil is maybe lying to God.
Or better, lying to love.

49

The priest shakes his head.
He doesn't comprehend.

But the priest understands
when I tell him that I want to
pour gasoline over my evil body
and light it,
He says, "That's more like it!
That kind of evil!"
(Evil it seems comes in brands,
like soup or detergent.)

Ms. Dog,
why is you evil?
It climbed into me.
It didn't mean to.

Maybe my mother cut the God out of me
when I was two in my playpen.
Is it too late, too late
to open the incision and plant Him there again?
All is wilderness.
All is hay that died from too much rain,
my stinky tears.
Whose God are you looking for? asked the priest.
I replied:
a starving man doesn't ask what the meal is.
I would eat a tomato, or a fire bird or music.
I would eat a moth soaked in vinegar.
But is there any food anywhere,
in the wind's hat?
in the sea's olive?

Is it true?
Is it true?

I wouldn't mind if God were wooden,
I'd wear Him like a house,
praise His knot holes,
shine Him like a shoe.
I would not let Him burn.
I would not burn myself
for I would be wearing Him.
Oh wood, my father, my shelter,
bless you.

Bless all useful objects,
the spoons made of bone,
the mattress I cook my dreams upon,
the typewriter that is my church
with an altar of keys always waiting,
the ladders that let us climb,
both fireman and roofer.
Bless also the skillet,
black and oil-soaked,
that fries eggs like the eyes of saints.
Bless the shoe for holding my foot
and letting me walk with the omnipotence
of a cat over glass or dog shit.
Bless the lights for going on
giving me eyes like two small cameras.
Is it true?

If all this can be
then why am I in this country of black mud?

and the land shall become blazing pitch, which night
and day shall never be quenched, and its smoke shall
go up forever. From generation to generation it shall
lie waste and no man shall pass through it ever again.

Yet I pass through.
I pass through.
On the northern shore of Lake Galilee
Jesus and John preached to the local fishermen.

Yet I am not a fisherman.
I pass through.
I pass through.
The sun is black mud.
The moon becomes a blood ball.
If religion were a dream, someone said,
then it were still a dream worth dreaming.
True! True!
I whisper to my wood walls.

The state Capitol of Boston
has a gold dome.
During the War,
the one I grew up in,
they painted out the gold.
What did they think the Nazis
would do with it,
make it into teeth?
Peel it off and buy whores?
Wrap the Mayor up in it like a mummy
and put him on display in the Public Gardens?

In heaven,
there will be a secret door,
there will be flowers with eyes that wink,
there will be light flowing from a bronze bell,
there will be as much love as there
are cunners off the coast of Maine,
there will be gold that no one hides
from the Nazis,
there will be statues that the angel
inside of Michelangelo's hand fashioned.
I will lay open my soul
and hear an answer.
Hello. Hello. It will call back,
"Here's a butter knife," it will say.
"So scrape off your hunger and the mud."
But is it true?
Is it true?

My tongue is slit.
It cannot eat.
Even if I were a king,
with a whole tongue,
I would be put to death with a shovel.
True, I have friends,
a few,
each one is a soul in two bodies.
Each one is a man or a woman.

Let me now praise
the male of our species,
let me praise men,
and their eggs of courage,

their fine lives of the cock,
their awful lives in the office.
Let me praise men for eating the apple
and finding woman
like a big brain of coral.

Let me praise humans,
praise the men of God.
The men of God are God.

From the Tamil, I read,
"The rock that resists the crowbar
gives way to the roots of the tender plant."
I read this and go to sleep
and when I wake
Nixon will have declared the Vietnam war
is over. No more deaths, body by body.
(But this will be such old news
before you read my words.
Old and senile.)
Still I will hear this and will be happy,
happy kind of,
for I know there will be more wars
and more deaths
and then the headlines will be no more than a petal
upon a crater.
Deep earth,
redeem us from our redeemers.
Keep us, God, far from our politicians
and keep us near to the grape that wakes us up.
Keep us near to the wolf of death.
Keep us near to the wife of the sun.

Is it true?
Is it true?

Never mind.
I'll do my own wash.

I have,
for some time,
called myself,
Ms. Dog.
Why?
Because I am almost animal
and yet the animal I lost most —
that animal is near to God,
but lost from Him.
Do you understand?
Can you read my hieroglyphics?
No language is perfect.
I only know English.
English is not perfect.
When I tell the priest I am full
of bowel movement, right into the fingers,
he shrugs. To him shit is good.
To me, to my mother, it was poison
and the poison was all of me
in the nose, in the ears, in the lungs.
That's why language fails.
Because to one, shit is a feeder of plants,
to another the evil that permeates them
and although they try,
day after day of childhood,
they can't push the poison out.

So much for language.
So much for psychology.
God lives in shit — I have been told.
I believe both.
Is it true?
Is it true?

> *Do you not know, have you not heard, were you not told
> long ago, have you not perceived ever since the world
> began that God sits throned on the vaulted roof of
> earth, whose inhabitants are like grasshoppers?*

Grasshoppers
and me one of them,
my eight legs like crutches.
Bless the animals of this earth,
the wolf in its hiding spoon,
the fly in its tiny life,
the fish in its fragrance I lost,
The Genghis dog of the Serengeti
that kills its baby
because it was born to kill,
born to pound out life like flour,
the mouse and the rat for the vermin
and disease that they must put up with,
all, all, bless them,
bless them,
lest they die without God.

Bless also, vegetable,
trees, the sea without which there is no mother,
the earth without which there is no father,
no flowers that grow out of rock.

Is it true?
Is it true?
I can only imagine it is true
that Jesus comes with his eggful of miracles,
his awful death, his blackboard full of graffiti.
Maybe I'm dead now
and have found Him.
Maybe my evil body is done with.
For I look up,
and in a blaze of butter is
Christ,
soiled with my sour tears,
Christ,
a lamb that has been slain,
his guts drooping like a sea worm,
but who lives on, lives on
like the wings of an Atlantic seagull.
Though he has stopped flying,
the wings go on flapping
despite it all,
despite it all.

WELCOME MORNING

There is joy
in all:
in the hair I brush each morning,
in the Cannon towel, newly washed,
that I rub my body with each morning,
in the chapel of eggs I cook
each morning,
in the outcry from the kettle
that heats my coffee
each morning,
in the spoon and the chair
that cry "hello there, Anne"
each morning,
in the godhead of the table
that I set my silver, plate, cup upon
each morning.

All this is God,
right here in my pea-green house
each morning
and I mean,
though often forget,
to give thanks,
to faint down by the kitchen table
in a prayer of rejoicing

as the holy birds at the kitchen window
peck into their marriage of seeds.

So while I think of it,
let me paint a thank-you on my palm
for this God, this laughter of the morning,
lest it go unspoken.

The Joy that isn't shared, I've heard,
dies young.

JESUS, THE ACTOR, PLAYS THE HOLY GHOST

Oh, Mother,
Virgin Mother,
before the gulls take me out the door,
marry me.
Marry me not to a goat
but to a goddess.
What?
You say it can not be done!

Then I will do it!
I wash the crows
but they do not whiten.
I push out the desk,
pulling it from its roots.
I shave the caterpillar
but he is only a worm.
I take the yellow papers
and I write on them
but they crumble like men's ashes.
I take the daisy
and blow my heart into it
but it will not speak.

Oh, mother,
marry me,
before the gulls take me out the door.

Will I marry the dark earth,
the thief of the daylight?
Will I marry a tree
and only wave my hands at you
from your front yard?
Oh, mother,
oh, mother,
you marry me,
save me from the cockroach,
weave me into the sun.
There will be bread.
There will be water.
My elbows will be salt.

Oh, Mary,
Gentle Mother,
open the door and let me in.
A bee has stung your belly with faith.
Let me float in it like a fish.
Let me in! Let me in!
I have been born many times, a false Messiah,
but let me be born again
into something true.

THE GOD-MONGER

With all my questions,
all the nihilistic words in my head,
I went in search of an answer,
I went in search of the other world
which I reached by digging underground,
past the stones as solemn as preachers,
past the roots, throbbing like veins
and went in search of some animal of wisdom,
and went in search, it could be said,
of my husband (i.e. the one who carries you through).

Down.
Down.
Down.
There I found a mouse
with trees growing out of his belly.
He was all wise.
He was my husband.
Yet he was silent.

He did three things.
He extruded a gourd of water.
Then I hit him on the head,
gently, a hit more like a knock.
Then he extruded a gourd of beer.
I knocked once more
and finally a dish of gravy.

Those were my answers.
Water. Beer. Food.
I was not satisfied.

Though the mouse
had not licked my leprous skin
that was my final answer.

The soul was not cured,
it was as full as a clothes closet
of dresses that did not fit.
Water. Beer. Gravy.
It simply had to be enough.
Husband,
who am I to reject the naming of foods
in a time of famine?

WHAT THE BIRD WITH THE HUMAN HEAD KNEW

I went to the bird
with the human head,
and asked,
Please Sir,
where is God?

God is too busy
to be here on earth,
His angels are like
one thousand geese assembled
and always flapping.
But I can tell you where the well of God is.

Is it on earth?
I asked.
He replied,
Yes. It was dragged down
from paradise by one of the geese.

I walked many days,
past witches that eat grandmothers knitting booties
as if they were collecting a debt.
Then, in the middle of the desert
I found the well,
it bubbled up and down like a litter of cats
and there was water,

and I drank,
and there was water,
and I drank.

Then the well spoke to me.
It said: Abundance is scooped from abundance,
yet abundance remains.

Then I knew.

THE FIRE THIEF

It began with begging.
In the beginning it was all God's icebox
and everyone ate raw fish or animals
and there was no fire at night to dance to,
no fire at day to cook by.

Everyone was two years old.
Yet they tried,
how they tried,
to get the fire:
the vultures tried, the coyote tried, the rabbit
tried; the spider tried
and almost made it back with a balloon
of fire on his back.

First the crow had it,
then a wren stole it,
then a hawk stole it,
and set the whole land on fire,
making the land as treeless as a dinner plate.
Nevertheless, it went out.
Maybe the bee went out of it?
Maybe it was killed by the tears of God?

Next a water rat and a codfish had it,
cooking their mussels every day,

but it went out.
Maybe the mussels were cross.

Next a human killed a snake with a yam-stick
and fire bloomed like a scar from its mouth.
But it went out.
The snake in it died.

A woman came
with six fingers
and in the extra finger was fire
and she gave it away like a kiss.
But it went out.
Maybe the skin of the finger undressed.

Next another woman had it,
she could take fire from between her legs
and she gave it to one man.
But it went out.
Maybe he thought touching was an act of war,
and he pissed on it in disgust.

Next it was stolen from God while He was sleeping
by the soldiers of the sun.
But it went out.
The soldiers of the sun now hide in volcanoes.

Next crafty Prometheus stole it from heaven
and for this deed his liver and heart were eaten each day.
So in due course it went out.
With each liver, each heart,
it grew fainter.
Maybe it could not bloom in the death house.

Then a dog went up to God,
he swam through the sky,
and when he got there he pleaded
and God said, *Take it! Take it!*
But keep it sacred.
and the dog came down and gave it to many men
saying:
Hide the fire!
Hide the fire!

They did not listen forever
for they burned Joan
and many, and many,
burned at the stake,
peeling their skin off,
boiling their good red blood,
their hearts like eggs,
and the great house of God was wrong
to give the fire to the dog,
and the great house of God will never forget it,
and each day, asks the sea,
its mother,
to forgive,
to forgive.

THE BIG HEART

*"Too many things are occurring for even
a big heart to hold."* From an essay by W. B. Yeats

Big heart,
wide as a watermelon,
but wise as birth,
there is so much abundance
in the people I have:
Max, Lois, Joe, Louise,
Joan, Marie, Dawn,
Arlene, Father Dunne,
and all in their short lives
give to me repeatedly,
in the way the sea
places its many fingers on the shore,
again and again
and they know me,
they help me unravel,
they listen with ears made of conch shells,
they speak back with the wine of the best region.
They are my staff.
They comfort me.

They hear how
the artery of my soul has been severed
and soul is spurting out upon them,
bleeding on them,
messing up their clothes,
dirtying their shoes.

And God is filling me,
though there are times of doubt
as hollow as the Grand Canyon,
still God is filling me.
He is giving me the thoughts of dogs,
the spider in its intricate web,
the sun
in all its amazement,
and a slain ram
that is the glory,
the mystery of great cost,
and my heart,
which is very big,
I promise it is very large,
a monster of sorts,
takes it all in —
all in comes the fury of love.

WORDS

Be careful of words,
even the miraculous ones.
For the miraculous we do our best,
sometimes they swarm like insects
and leave not a sting but a kiss.
They can be as good as fingers.
They can be as trusty as the rock
you stick your bottom on.
But they can be both daisies and bruises.

Yet I am in love with words.
They are doves falling out of the ceiling.
They are six holy oranges sitting in my lap.
They are the trees, the legs of summer,
and the sun, its passionate face.

Yet often they fail me.
I have so much I want to say,
so many stories, images, proverbs, etc.
But the words aren't good enough,
the wrong ones kiss me.
Sometimes I fly like an eagle
but with the wings of a wren.

But I try to take care
and be gentle to them.
Words and eggs must be handled with care.
Once broken they are impossible
things to repair.

MOTHERS

for J.B.

Oh mother,
here in your lap,
as good as a bowlful of clouds,
I your greedy child
am given your breast,
the sea wrapped in skin,
and your arms,
roots covered with moss
and with new shoots sticking out
to tickle the laugh out of me.
Yes, I am wedded to my teddy
but he has the smell of you
as well as the smell of me.
Your necklace that I finger
is all angel eyes.
Your rings that sparkle
are like the moon on the pond.
Your legs that bounce me up and down,
your dear nylon-covered legs,
are the horses I will ride
into eternity.

Oh mother,
after this lap of childhood
I will never go forth

into the big people's world
as an alien,
a fabrication,
or falter
when someone else
is as empty as a shoe.

DOCTORS

They work with herbs
and penicillin.
They work with gentleness
and the scalpel.
They dig out the cancer,
close an incision
and say a prayer
to the poverty of the skin.
They are not Gods
though they would like to be;
they are only a human
trying to fix up a human.
Many humans die.
They die like the tender,
palpitating berries
in November.
But all along the doctors remember:
First do no harm.
They would kiss if it would heal.
It would not heal.

If the doctors cure
then the sun sees it.
If the doctors kill
then the earth hides it.

The doctors should fear arrogance
more than cardiac arrest.
If they are too proud,
and some are,
then they leave home on horseback
but God returns them on foot.

FRENZY

I am not lazy.
I am on the amphetamine of the soul.
I am, each day,
typing out the God
my typewriter believes in.
Very quick. Very intense,
like a wolf at a live heart.
Not lazy.
When a lazy man, they say,
looks toward heaven,
the angels close the windows.

Oh angels,
keep the windows open
so that I may reach in
and steal each object,
objects that tell me the sea is not dying,
objects that tell me the dirt has a life-wish,
that the Christ who walked for me,
walked on true ground
and that this frenzy,
like bees stinging the heart all morning,
will keep the angels
with their windows open,
wide as an English bathtub.

SNOW

Snow,
blessed snow,
comes out of the sky
like bleached flies.
The ground is no longer naked.
The ground has on its clothes.
The trees poke out of sheets
and each branch wears the sock of God.

There is hope.
There is hope everywhere.
I bite it.
Someone once said:
Don't bite till you know
if it's bread or stone.
What I bite is all bread,
rising, yeasty as a cloud.

There is hope.
There is hope everywhere.
Today God gives milk
and I have the pail.

SMALL WIRE

My faith
is a great weight
hung on a small wire,
as doth the spider
hang her baby on a thin web,
as doth the vine,
twiggy and wooden,
hold up grapes
like eyeballs,
as many angels
dance on the head of a pin.

God does not need
too much wire to keep Him there,
just a thin vein,
with blood pushing back and forth in it,
and some love.
As it has been said:
Love and a cough
cannot be concealed.
Even a small cough.
Even a small love.
So if you have only a thin wire,
God does not mind.
He will enter your hands
as easily as ten cents used to
bring forth a Coke.

THE SAINTS COME MARCHING IN

(With thanks and gratitude to Phyllis McGinley
for her book of the lives of the Saints.)

The Saints come,
as human as a mouth,
with a bag of God in their backs,
like a hunchback,
they come,
they come marching in.
They come
crowding together
like the devout baseball fans
at a game.
Their game is taking God literally,
taking Him at His word,
though often He be mute.

Catherine of Sienna,
the illiterate girl who lectured to Popes,
each word a flower,
yet hung out cold in its loneliness.

Saint Augustine said:
God, make me chaste,
but not yet.
The party had not begun.
The food was there, the drinks were there
but the people were waiting at the door
to be let in,

waiting as Augustine was waiting
with their open mouths
like the beaks of nestlings.

Teresa of Ávila said:
I have no defense against affection.
I could be bribed with a sardine.
Oh dear Teresa,
I could be bribed likewise.
The hand in mine,
or the chapel inside a bean.

Elisha,
an early Desert Father,
who caroled like a thrush
three hundred thousand songs.
I am not a saint
but I carol with what the typewriter gives,
with what God gives,
as even He gives the hair on our heads.

Nicholas the Pilgrim,
a shepherd
who kept his sheep calm
by singing to them
Kyrie eleison.
The sheep or the horse,
numb as the moon,
need God to be sung unto them.
The dog needs it too.
He is sick of dead bodies.

Saints have no moderation,
nor do poets,
just exuberance.

Ávilan of Teresa
who taught her nuns
to dance for joy
in the cloister,
a dance of Joy,
unto God,
as the birds fling
themselves into the air,
as the human face moves
knowing it will be kissed.

Blessed Bertilla Boscardin,
called "the goose"
in the Italian village of Brendola.
"I am a goose," she said,
"but teach me to be a saint."
There among the pots and pans
of potato peelings
she arrived at her goal.

Vincent Pallotti
who many times came home
half naked
because he had parted with his clothes.
When one gives one's clothes
one says "good morning."
When one gives one's clothes
one gives the suit of Jehovah.

Saint Paul said to the Galatians:
There is neither Jew nor Greek,
there is neither male nor female,
for ye are all . . . heirs according
to the promise.
He knew that each fish
was given paradise
in its slimy skin,
in its little gasping kiss of the sea.

And I who have visited many beds
and never belonged in one
speak of
Saint Dominic who in his happy poverty
had to die in Brother Moneta's bed
because he had none of his own.

No matter whose bed you die in
the bed will be yours
for your voyage
onto the surgical andiron
of God.

NOT SO. NOT SO.

I cannot walk an inch
without trying to walk to God.
I cannot move a finger
without trying to touch God.
Perhaps it is this way:
He is in the graves of the horses.
He is in the swarm, the frenzy of the bees.
He is in the tailor mending my pantsuit.
He is in Boston, raised up by the skyscrapers.
He is in the bird, that shameless flyer.
He is in the potter who makes clay into a kiss.

Heaven replies:
Not so! Not so!

I say thus and thus
and heaven smashes my words.

Is not God in the hiss of the river?

Not so! Not so!

Is not God in the ant heap,
stepping, clutching, dying, being born?

Not so! Not so!

Where then?
I cannot move an inch.

Look to your heart
that flutters in and out like a moth.
God is not indifferent to your need.
You have a thousand prayers
but God has one.

THE ROWING ENDETH

I'm mooring my rowboat
at the dock of the island called God.
This dock is made in the shape of a fish
and there are many boats moored
at many different docks.
"It's okay," I say to myself,
with blisters that broke and healed
and broke and healed —
saving themselves over and over.
And salt sticking to my face and arms like
a glue-skin pocked with grains of tapioca.
I empty myself from my wooden boat
and onto the flesh of The Island.

"On with it!" He says and thus
we squat on the rocks by the sea
and play —— can it be true ——
a game of poker.
He calls me.
I win because I hold a royal straight flush.
He wins because He holds five aces.
A wild card had been announced
but I had not heard it
being in such a state of awe
when He took out the cards and dealt.
As he plunks down His five aces

and I sit grinning at my royal flush,
He starts to laugh,
the laughter rolling like a hoop out of His mouth
and into mine,
and such laughter that He doubles right over me
laughing a Rejoice-Chorus at our two triumphs.
Then I laugh, the fishy dock laughs
the sea laughs. The Island laughs.
The Absurd laughs.

Dearest dealer,
I with my royal straight flush,
love you so for your wild card,
that untamable, eternal, gut-driven *ha-ha*
and lucky love.